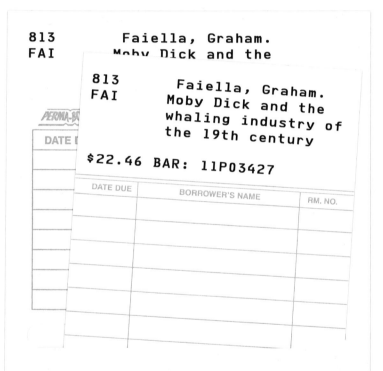

813
FAI   Faiella, Graham.
Moby Dick and the

$22.46

CLARK MIDDLE/HIGH
SCHOOL
1921 DAVIS AVENUE
WHITING, IN 46394

Moby Dick and the Whaling Industry of the 19th Century

Graham Faiella

rosen central
Primary Source™

The Rosen Publishing Group, Inc., New York

Published in 2004 by The Rosen Publishing Group, Inc.
29 East 21st Street, New York, NY 10010

Unless otherwise attributed, all quotes in this book are excerpted from *Moby Dick*.

Library of Congress Cataloging-in-Publication Data

Faiella, Graham.
Moby Dick and the whaling industry of the 19th century/by Graham Faiella.—1st ed.
      p. cm.—(Looking at literature through primary sources)
Summary: Traces the process and influences behind the writing of Herman Melville's novel, *Moby Dick*, which was published in the 1850s and based on the author's own experience at sea. Includes bibliographical references and index.
ISBN 0-8239-4505-7 (library binding)
1. Melville, Herman, 1819–1891. *Moby Dick*. 2. Whaling—New England—History—19th century. 3. Sea stories, American—History and criticism. 4. Whaling in literature. 5. Whales in literature. [1. Melville, Herman, 1819–1891. *Moby Dick*. 2. Whaling—New England—History—19th century. 3. Sea stories—History and criticism. 4. Whaling in literature. 5. Whales in literature.]
I. Title. II. Series.
PS2384.M62F35 2004
813'.3—dc22

2003015893

Manufactured in the United States of America

On the cover: At top, an 1860s portrait of Herman Melville; at bottom left, a photograph of whalers cutting into blubber; and at bottom right, the title page of the original edition of *Moby Dick*.

CONTENTS

INTRODUCTION

Herman Melville, aged twenty-one, set sail from Fairhaven, Massachusetts, as an ordinary seaman on the whaling ship *Acushnet*. It was January 1841. His whaling experiences from that voyage became the backbone of his whaling epic, *Moby Dick: or, The Whale*. Melville wrote *Moby Dick* by splicing his personal experience of whaling with what he read and learned about it from books. The result is an extraordinary work of fiction, seasoned with imagination, fact, and fantasy. Melville himself recognized that, although the book was about "a whaling voyage," he needed to "cook the thing up." As he said, "blubber is blubber," but "I mean to give the truth of the thing [whaling], [in] spite of this."

New England whaling from Massachusetts ports such as New Bedford and Nantucket peaked in 1846, just five years before the publication of *Moby Dick*. Whales were already becoming scarce.

In the 1860s, the first steam-powered whaling ships were built. In 1868, the explosive harpoon was invented, eliminating

THE SPERMACETI WHALE

This nineteenth-century engraving depicts a spermaceti, or sperm, whale, the type of whale portrayed by Herman Melville in *Moby Dick*. The sperm whale's head, known as the melon, can be as long as one-third of its body and typically accounts for one-quarter of its weight.

the need for hand-thrown harpoons. Crude oil was becoming a more economical substitute for whale oil. By the time Melville died in 1891, nineteenth-century whaling in America was virtually dead, too. But Melville's fame was resurrected in the early twentieth century when *Moby Dick* became acknowledged as an epic story of Yankee whaling and a masterpiece of American literature.

Chapter 1

The Life of Herman Melville

In the early 1800s, America was a young country. The Declaration of Independence had been signed in 1776. In 1820, there were just twenty-two states in the Union. The population of the country was less than 10 million. The American West was "wild." Even the Great Lakes area was still wilderness, inhabited mainly by Native Americans.

Slavery was a critical issue between southern and northern states. America was adolescent in the 1800s. This was a century of geographical expansion, the Industrial Revolution, and the evolution of political parties. It was in this melting pot of growth, reform, struggle, and the search for self-identity that Herman Melville lived and wrote *Moby Dick*.

Herman Melville was born on August 1, 1819, in New York City, to Maria Gansevoort and Allan Melville. He was the third of eight children. Herman's father had traveled widely as a young man. He once estimated that he had traveled nearly the distance of the earth's circumference by land and twice as far by sea.

◆◆◆ Painted by Asa W. Twitchell, this is a portrait of Herman Melville as a young man, created perhaps around the time he first served as a crew member on a ship.

Money was a constant problem for the Melville family. In 1830, Allan Melville was forced by debts to close his import business in New York City and move the family to Albany, New York. Allan Melville died early in 1832.

Herman originally planned to become a teacher. But when his family moved to Lansingburgh (now Troy), New York, he enrolled at the Lansingburgh Academy to study engineering and surveying. He later applied for a job on the Erie Canal, but he did not get the job. In June 1839, Herman sailed as a crew member on the merchant ship *St. Lawrence* from New York to Liverpool, England, and back. It was his first taste of life at sea. In the summer of 1840, Herman and a friend traveled out West to visit his uncle Thomas in Galena, Illinois, and to look for work.

Melville Goes Whaling

Finding no work in the West, Melville returned to New York to the same old problems: no job, family debts, and, in the case of his mother and brother, poor health. In Galena, Melville heard stories about his cousin Thomas's whaling voyages to the South Seas. He decided that he, too, would go whaling. In January 1841, Melville sailed as an ordinary seaman on the whaling ship *Acushnet*.

Ishmael, the narrator of *Moby Dick*, believes that his destiny is to go whaling. He echoes the author's own experience of the sea:

> **But wherefore it was that after having repeatedly smelt the sea as a merchant sailor, I should now take it into my head to go on a whaling voyage; this the invisible police officer of the Fates, who has the constant surveillance of me, and secretly dogs me, and influences me in some unaccountable way—he can better answer than anyone else. And, doubtless, my going on this whaling voyage, formed part of the grand programme of Providence that was drawn up a long time ago.**

Jumping Ship and Other Adventures

Deserting the ship at Nuku Hiva, in the Marquesas Islands, in June 1842, Melville and a shipmate spent a month living

among the native Typee people. In August, they joined an Australian whaling ship, the *Lucy Ann*. At Tahiti, Melville and other *Lucy Ann* crew members were jailed for mutiny. In Tahiti, as on Nuku Hiva, Melville's experience of the simple life of the "uncivilized" native islanders hardened his attitude against "civilized" man.

He and his friend Toby escaped to the nearby island of Moorea. From there, Melville signed on the Nantucket whaling ship *Charles and Henry*, probably as a harpooner.

Melville left the ship at Lahaina, on the island of Maui in the Sandwich Islands (now Hawaii), in May 1843. In Honolulu, Melville worked as a clerk in a general store. There he sympathized with the native Hawaiians whose low status he shared as a "common sailor." He was equally offended by the negative effects of "civilization" on the islanders, including the destructive influence of missionaries.

In August 1843, Melville enlisted as an ordinary seaman on a U.S. Navy frigate, the *United States*. Melville hated the brutal military discipline on the ship. He had long conversations about literature, philosophy, and life with some of the other crew. Melville later wrote that, in one particularly intense literary discussion during a night watch, he "learned more than he had ever done in any single night since." In *Moby Dick* he wrote, "a whale-ship was my Yale College and my Harvard."

An Incident to Remember

One incident might have taken root in his memory. The ship's cooper (barrel maker or woodworker) was pulled overboard one day by the hammock he was washing, and he drowned. A few days before, a sailor had accused the cooper of making life buoys that leaked. The cooper had replied that a man should drown if he could not save himself with his own life buoy. Melville includes many ominous incidents like this in *Moby Dick*, foreshadowing the fate of the *Pequod* and its crew. In *Moby Dick*, the carpenter makes a life buoy out of the coffin of Queequeg (pronounced KWEE-kway), the *Pequod*'s chief harpooner.

> **"A life-buoy of a coffin!" cried Starbuck, starting. "Rather queer, that, I should say," said Stubb. "It will make a good enough one," said Flask, "the carpenter here can arrange it easily."**

Native of Nukahiva

WILEY & PUTNAM'S

LIBRARY OF

AMERICAN BOOKS.

TYPEE:

A PEEP AT POLYNESIAN LIFE.

PART I.

At top is a drawing by J. A. Atkinson of a native of Nuka Hiva, one of the Marquesas Islands. In *Typee: A Peep at Polynesian Life*, the title page of which is shown at bottom, Herman Melville offered a fictionalized version of his adventures on the Marquesas Islands. The book was a success with American and English readers who were intrigued by stories of foreign places.

Returning Home

Back home, Melville found his mother still in financial difficulties. He realized he would have to earn money from writing. His first book was *Typee*, in which he combined recollections of his life among the Typee on Nuku Hiva, narratives from other sources, and his own imagination. Melville would use the

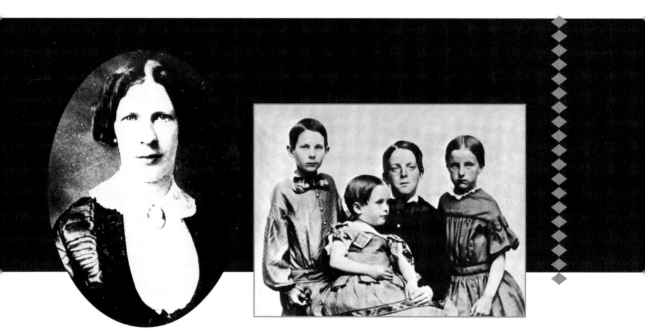

At left, a portrait of Elizabeth Shaw, whom Herman Melville married in 1847. At right, their four children: Stanwix, Frances, Malcolm, and Elizabeth.

same combination of fact and fantasy to write all his books, including *Moby Dick*.

Family and Earning a Living

In August 1847, Melville married Elizabeth Shaw from Boston, the daughter of Judge Lemuel Shaw, chief justice of the Supreme Judicial Court of Massachusetts between 1830 and 1860. Debts forced Melville to continue writing. He completed his third book, *Mardi*, in May 1848. The next, *Redburn*, was based on his voyage to Liverpool in the summer of 1839. He based *White Jacket* on the time he spent as a navy seaman on the U. S. Navy frigate *United States*. Melville had made a white jacket during the voyage, to keep warm while the ship was in the cold southern seas around Cape Horn.

Melville's first child, Malcolm, was born in February 1849. Late that same year, Melville traveled to England and other parts of Europe to gather personal experiences for a new book he had in mind. On the voyage to England, he saw ball lightning (also called corpusants, or Saint Elmo's fire) for the first time. He describes a similar incident in *Moby Dick*.

"Look aloft!" cried Starbuck. "The corpusants! the corpusants!" All the yard-arms were tipped with a pallid fire; and touched at each tri-pointed lightning-rod-end with three tapering white flames, each of the three tall masts was silently burning . . .

Melville returned to New York in February 1850. His friend Richard Henry Dana suggested that he write a book that would "do for the whaling industry what he had done for the naval service in *White Jacket* and what Dana had done for the merchant marine in *Two Years Before the Mast*."

In June 1850, Melville wrote to his English publisher, Richard Bentley, about his plans for *Moby Dick*. "The book is a romance of adventure founded upon certain wild legends in the Southern Sperm Whale Fisheries, and illustrated by the author's own personal experience, of two years and more, as a harpooner." Melville, of course, did not have experience of "two years and more, as a harpooner." It was more like a few months.

Writing *Moby Dick*

In September 1850, Melville moved the family from New York to a farm near Pittsfield, Massachusetts. He wrote *Moby Dick* in a little more than a year, between the summer of 1850 and September 1851. The climax of the story (the attack and sinking of the whale ship *Pequod* by the white whale Moby Dick) was based on a true incident. In 1820, the whale ship *Essex* sank after being attacked by a huge sperm whale in the Pacific Ocean. Melville had known this story at least since his days on the *Acushnet*, if not earlier.

Moby Dick received mixed critical reviews and did not sell well. Melville would have to keep writing to pay the bills.

Melville's second son, Stanwix, was born in October 1851. In July 1852, Melville traveled to New Bedford, Nantucket, and Martha's Vineyard. It was his first visit to Nantucket.

Melville's Later Years

In 1863, Melville moved back to New York City. In 1866, at age forty-seven, he was still short of money and still in debt. He needed a secure income. In December that year, he started working as a customs officer for New York City. He continued to write poetry and short stories, but his job, which paid him four dollars a day, provided financial security.

Melville spent almost twenty years as a New York customs inspector. He retired in 1885. In 1888, he started, but did not finish, his last major work, the novel *Billy Budd*.

In the early hours of September 28, 1891, at the age of seventy-two, Herman Melville died. At the time of his death he was recognized as a distinguished author. But his books were not popular. He had a following of admirers, but not fame. Popular acclaim would come from the 1920s onward.

Chapter 2

Moby Dick: The Story

The narrator of *Moby Dick* is Ishmael, who has decided that he will "sail about a little and see the watery part of the world." He "takes it into [his] head" to go on a whaling voyage. He starts by describing the "insular [island] city of the Manhattoes [Manhattan, New York City]." Melville was born in New York City, so he knew the places he was describing very well.

Ishmael heads for the whaling port of New Bedford, Massachusetts. There, he stops overnight at the Spouter Inn. He has to share his bed with the whaling harpooner Queequeg, a "wild cannibal" from a South Seas island in the Pacific. Ishmael and Queequeg soon become friends.

They board "the packet [passenger ship]" for Nantucket where they "sign articles" to join a whaling ship, the *Pequod*. Queequeg demonstrates his harpooning skill to the two part-owners of the *Pequod*, Captain Peleg and Captain Bildad. Both are retired Nantucket Quaker whalemen. Queequeg is made chief harpooner on the *Pequod*.

This is a view of Manhattan, New York, as seen by the artist J. W. Hill in 1848, two years before Herman Melville began writing *Moby Dick*. Melville used Manhattan, where he was born, as the basis for the city of Manhottoes in *Moby Dick*.

The Crew of the *Pequod*

The ship sets sail on "a short, cold Christmas" day. The officers (headsmen) and crew of the *Pequod* are introduced to the reader. Starbuck, chief mate, is a Quaker "by descent" from Nantucket. Stubb, second mate, is from Cape Cod. Flask, third mate, is from Martha's Vineyard, the island near Nantucket. Queequeg, the *Pequod*'s chief harpooner, is chosen by Starbuck to be his squire (assistant). Tashtego, another harpooner, is "an unmixed [pure] Indian" from Gay Head on Martha's Vineyard

♦♦♦ Captain Ahab is depicted in this illustration from a 1923 edition of *Moby Dick*. Ahab made it clear that he was master of his ship. He told one of his crew members, "there is one God that is Lord over the earth, and one captain that is lord over the *Pequod*."

(and therefore a "Gay-Header"). Stubb chooses Tashtego to be his squire. The third harpooner is Daggoo, "a gigantic, coal-black negro-savage" from Africa, squire to the third mate "little Flask, who looked like a chess-man beside him." The rest of the crew are mainly from "all the isles of the seas," because "Islanders seem to make the best whalemen."

Ahab is the captain of the *Pequod*. One of his legs was bitten off by a sperm whale. In its place he wears a leg "fashioned from the polished bone of the sperm whale's jaw." Captain Ahab offers a one-ounce gold coin, which he nails to the mast, to the first person who sees the white whale called Moby Dick. Starbuck asks if it was Moby Dick that bit off Ahab's leg. "Aye, Starbuck; aye, my hearties all round; it was Moby Dick that dismasted me; Moby Dick that brought me to this dead stump I stand on now," says Ahab. From this point the crew members know that their whaling voyage is also Ahab's search to take revenge on Moby Dick.

Whale Chart, prepared by U.S. Navy oceanographer Matthew Maury, shows a concentration of sperm whales (denoted in pink) in the Pacific Ocean in 1851.

The Route of the *Pequod*

The *Pequod* sails through the Atlantic cruising (whaling) grounds where the crew catch some whales, then around the southern tip of Africa, the Cape of Good Hope. Off "the distant Crozetts" (cruising grounds around the Crozet Islands, southeast of Good Hope), they meet another whaling ship. During its entire voyage, the *Pequod* will meet a total of nine other whaling ships, including the *Rachel,* which rescues Ishmael at the end of the book.

From "the Crozetts" the *Pequod* continues toward Java, in the East Indies (Indonesia). At one point Daggoo thinks he sees "the White Whale," Moby Dick. They go after it, but it turns out to be the white body of "the great live squid" (giant squid), which soon disappears. The next day Stubb kills a whale and eats some of it for supper. Later, another whale is caught. They cut the whale up by the side of the ship. When they cut its head off, Tashtego falls into it as it sinks. Queequeg dives in and rescues him.

Into the Pacific

The *Pequod* sails through the Strait of Sunda, between the Indonesian islands of Sumatra and Java. Ahab is heading north, "to gain the far coast of Japan, in time for the great

◆◆◆ **This engraving shows what a typical eighteenth-century whaling ship looked like. The whaling ship was the crew's home away from home, as the typical voyage lasted for several years.**

whaling season there." Afterward the ship will head for "the Line [equator] in the Pacific" where Ahab "firmly counted upon giving battle to Moby Dick, in the sea he was most known to frequent." During this part of the voyage, Pip , a crewmember, falls overboard from a whaleboat while chasing a whale. He is rescued, but "from that hour the little negro went about the deck an idiot; such, at least, they said he was."

Later, Queequeg becomes sick with a fever. He "shuddered at the thought of being buried in his hammock" if he died. He wants to be buried at sea in "a canoe like those of Nantucket." He asks the carpenter to make him a coffin. He lies in it, with his harpoon, when it is finished. But "Queequeg suddenly rallied," decided he was not going to die, and instead "now used his coffin for a sea-chest." At the end of the book, Ishmael uses the coffin as a life buoy to stay afloat.

The *Pequod* sails into the Pacific and to the cruising grounds off Japan, where a typhoon strikes. Ahab decides to head for "the Line" to look for Moby Dick. As soon as they reach the cruising grounds of the Line, a lookout falls from the top of the mast. The ship's life buoy is thrown to the man, but he drowns, "swallowed up in the deep." The life buoy sinks. The carpenter prepares Queequeg's coffin to be the ship's new life buoy ("A life-buoy of a coffin!"). The next day they meet another whale ship, the *Rachel*. She is searching for a missing whaleboat and its crew. Captain Gardiner of the *Rachel* is desperate to find the missing crew because "My boy, my own boy is among them." Ahab refuses to

◆◆◆ This is an illustration from an article called "The Perils and Romance of Whaling," which was published in *The Century*, a quarterly journal, in 1890. It shows a crewman on the rig of a whaler announcing the sighting of a whale.

help look for the missing crew. The *Rachel* continues her search, "weeping for her children."

Meeting Moby Dick

Ahab is hoisted to the top of the mast to look out for Moby Dick. From there he is the first one to see the whale: "There she blows!—there she blows! A hump like a snow-hill! It is Moby Dick!"

The chase to kill Moby Dick takes place over three days. On the first day, Moby Dick snaps one of the whaleboats in two and eventually swims off. On the second day, the crew get three harpoons into Moby Dick. He smashes two boats with his flukes (tail). He flings the other one (Ahab's) over by "shooting perpendicularly from the sea" and tumbling it "over and over, into the air." One of the crew, "the Parsee," is missing.

On the third day, they lower the boats again when they see the spout of Moby Dick. The whale "came churning his tail among the boats; and once more flailed them apart . . . but leaving Ahab's almost without a scar." They see "lashed round and round to the fish's back . . . the half torn body of the Parsee." The wrecked boat crews return to the *Pequod*.

Moby Dick turns and attacks the ship, which begins to sink. Ahab, from his boat, manages to harpoon Moby Dick, but he gets tangled in the line. He is pulled to his death as the whale dives. The sinking ship creates a whirlpool that sucks down the ship, the crew, "and each floating oar, and every lance-pole, and spinning . . . all round and round in one vortex . . . out of sight."

◆◆◆ Moby Dick swims around the wrecked crew of the *Pequod* in this illustration from the novel. Captain Ahab's belief that whales acted out of malice and revenge was common among nineteenth-century seamen.

But, "one did survive the wreck." Ishmael, the narrator, is sucked toward the center of the vortex (whirlpool) but is saved when Queequeg's coffin life buoy floats to the surface. He hangs on until the next day. "On the second day, a sail drew near, nearer, and picked me up at last. It was . . . the 'Rachel,' that in her retracing search after her missing children, only found another orphan."

Whales and Whaling

Throughout the narrative of the voyage, Melville inserts chapters about whaling and whales. He describes the different kinds of whales, no matter how mistakenly ("I take the good old fashioned ground that the whale is a fish . . . a spouting fish with a horizontal tail. There you have him!"). Whales, of course, are mammals, not fish. In Melville's day, however, whale-men commonly called whales "fish."

He talks about famous sperm whales known to whalers at the time. He describes in detail how sperm whales are caught and the blubber cooked down ("tried out") into oil. He explains how the finest spermaceti oil is scooped out of the sperm whale's "case" (forehead compartment). He discusses "the honor and glory of whaling," and describes where ambergris comes from and other details about whales and whaling to fill out the narrative. In between, he includes references to religion, philosophy, mythology, history, and other people who write about whaling.

Chapter 3

Moby Dick: The Inspiration

Melville spent just two years of his life on whaling ships, from January 1841 until April 1843. His relatively skimpy whaling experience wasn't enough to fill out an epic whaling narrative such as *Moby Dick*. He had to fatten up the book by borrowing material from elsewhere. In the wreck of the whale ship *Essex* he found his main inspiration.

Owen Chase's *Narrative of the Wreck of the Whale-Ship* Essex

Under the command of Captain James Pollard, the *Essex* set sail from Nantucket on August 12, 1819. The *Essex* was hunting sperm whales in the Pacific, around the equator, when it was rammed by a big sperm whale and sank. The crew escaped in boats, sailing more than 4,000 miles (6,400 km) toward the coast of South America. Some of the crew were cannibalized by the others during their voyage. The survivors were picked up by passing ships. The details of the sinking of the *Essex* by a sperm whale and the fate of the surviving crew members were written

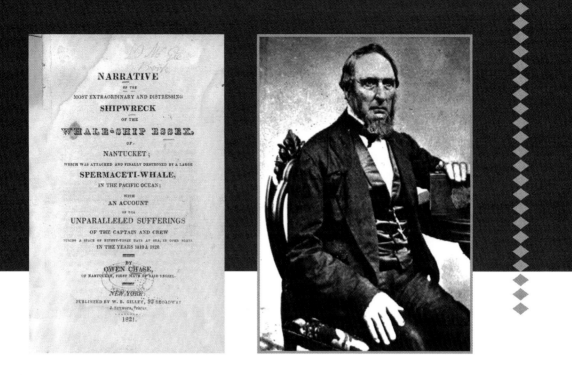

At left is the title page of *Narrative of the Shipwreck of the Whale-Ship* Essex by Owen Chase, who is pictured at right. Herman Melville found Chase's *Narrative* a bountiful resource while he was working on *Moby Dick.* Chase was twenty-two when the *Essex* was destroyed.

down by the ship's first mate, Owen Chase. His *Narrative of the Shipwreck of the Whale-Ship* Essex was published a year after the incident, in 1821.

On the *Acushnet*, during his whaling voyage of 1841, Melville and his shipmates talked about the *Essex* incident. Melville had a copy of the *Narrative* and made some notes in it, including the following: "When I was on board the ship *Acushnet* of Fairhaven, on the passage to the Pacific cruising-grounds, among other matters of forecastle conversations at times was the story of the

Essex. It was then that I first became acquainted with her history and her truly astounding fate."

It was the "truly astounding fate" of the *Essex* that provided Melville with the climax for *Moby Dick*. The manner of the whale's "revengeful" attack inspired the story about the search for a "powerful, knowing, and judiciously malicious" great sperm whale that destroys the ship as well as the captain and crew who have pursued it. Melville includes a summary of the *Essex* incident in *Moby Dick*, in his own words:

The Sperm Whale is in some cases sufficiently powerful, knowing, and judiciously malicious, as with direct aforethought [intent] to stave in, utterly destroy, and sink a large ship; and what is more, the Sperm Whale has done it. First: in the year 1820 the ship *Essex*, Captain Pollard, of Nantucket, was cruising in the Pacific Ocean. One day she saw spouts [of whales], lowered her boats, and gave chase to a shoal of sperm whales. Ere [before] long, several of the whales were wounded; when, suddenly, a very large whale escaping from the boats, issued from the shoal, and bore directly down upon the ship. Dashing his forehead against her hull, he so stove her in, that in less than "ten minutes" she settled down and fell over. Not a surviving plank of her has been seen since. After the severest exposure, part of the crew reached the land in their boats.

The Sinking of the *Essex*

The whale that sank the *Essex* attacked twice. Owen Chase described the first attack:

> I observed a very large spermaceti [sperm] whale, as well as I could judge, about eighty-five feet in length; he broke water about twenty rods [110 yards] off our weather bow, and was lying quietly, with his head in a direction for the ship. He spouted two or three times, and then disappeared. In less than two or three seconds he came up again, about the length of the ship off, and

Timeline

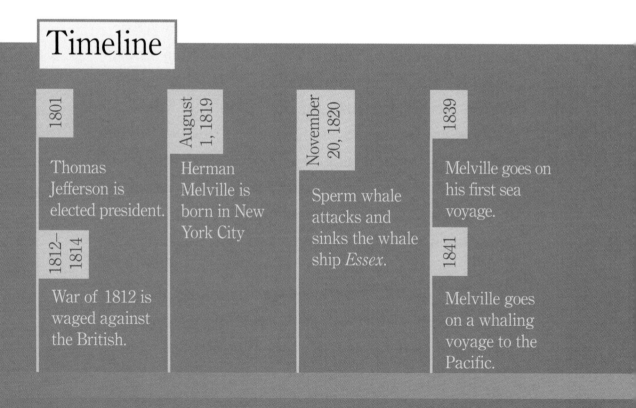

1801
Thomas Jefferson is elected president.

1812–1814
War of 1812 is waged against the British.

August 1, 1819
Herman Melville is born in New York City

November 20, 1820
Sperm whale attacks and sinks the whale ship *Essex*.

1839
Melville goes on his first sea voyage.

1841
Melville goes on a whaling voyage to the Pacific.

made directly for us, at the rate of about three knots. The ship was then going at about the same velocity . . . he came down upon us with full speed, and struck the ship with his head, just forward of the fore-chains [i.e., on the bow of the ship]; he gave us such an appalling and tremendous jar, as nearly threw us all on our faces . . . Many minutes elapsed before we were able to realize the dreadful accident; during which time he [the whale] passed under the ship, grazing her keel as he went along, came up alongside of her to leeward, & lay on top of the water."

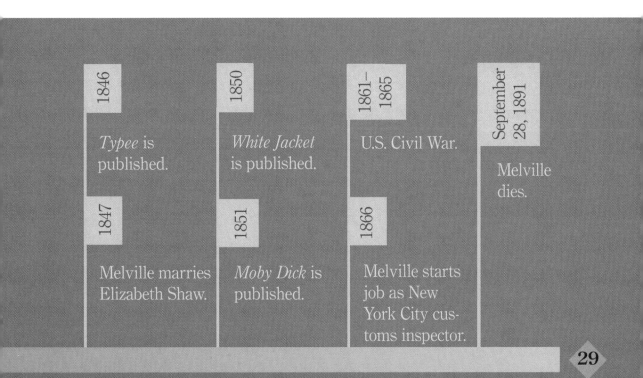

1846

Typee is published.

1847

Melville marries Elizabeth Shaw.

1850

White Jacket is published.

1851

Moby Dick is published.

1861–1865

U.S. Civil War.

1866

Melville starts job as New York City customs inspector.

September 28, 1891

Melville dies.

Shortly after, the whale attacked a second time:

I turned around, & saw him about one hundred rods [550 yards] directly ahead of us, coming down apparently with twice his ordinary speed . . . The surf flew in all directions about him, and his course towards us was marked by a white foam of a rod [5.5 yards] in width, which he made with the continual violent thrashing of his tail; his head was about half out of water, and in that way he came upon, and again struck the ship . . . He struck her to windward, directly under the cat-head, and completely stove in her bows.

Owen Chase reflects on the reason for the whale's attack: "His aspect was most horrible, and such as indicated resentment and fury. He came directly from the shoal which we had just before entered, and in which we had struck [harpooned] three of his companions, as if fired with revenge for their sufferings." The whale, he thought, deliberately attacked the ship "with direct aforethought," an act of revenge for the ship's harpooning of the whale's three "companions." As Melville says in *Moby Dick*: "I tell you, the sperm whale will stand no nonsense." Melville was most impressed with the apparent motive of revenge for the whale's attack on the *Essex*. Among other things, *Moby Dick* is a novel about revenge. In that, the sperm whale was the equal of Captain Ahab.

The Sinking of the *Pequod*

In the final pages of the novel, Melville describes the moment when Moby Dick begins to attack the *Pequod*.

> **Hearing the tremendous rush of the sea-crashing boat, the whale reeled round to present his blank forehead at bay; but in that evolution, catching sight of the nearing black hull of the ship; seemingly seeing in it the source of all his persecutions; bethinking it—it may be—a larger and nobler foe; of a sudden, he bore down upon its advancing prow, smiting his jaws amid fiery showers of foam.**

Shortly after, the whale's impact sinks the *Pequod*.

> **Retribution, swift vengeance, eternal malice were in his whole aspect, and spite of all that mortal man could do, the solid white buttress of his forehead smote the ship's starboard bow, till men and timbers reeled . . . Diving beneath the settling ship, the whale ran quivering along its keel; but turning under water, swiftly shot to the surface again, far off the other bow, but within a few yards of Ahab's boat, where, for a time, he lay quiescent [quiet].**

Melville spins out the climax of Ahab's encounter and battle with Moby Dick over three days of furious combat. By the third day, when the whale attacks the *Pequod* directly, the ship sinks almost immediately. The *Essex*, by contrast, was just going about her usual business of hunting whales on a sunny Pacific morning when, out of the blue, it was attacked by "a very large spermaceti whale." The *Essex* filled with water but remained afloat. The crew had time to collect provisions and useful navigation equipment from it. After about three days they abandoned the wreck, setting sail toward land in two boats. The ship was still afloat when they left it, unlike the splintered *Pequod* and its crew.

Mocha Dick and Other Fearsome Whales

Mocha Dick was a real whale, well known to whaling men in Melville's time. Described as "white as wool," he was named for Mocha Island, off the coast of Chile, where the whale was first sighted in 1810 by the crew of the *Penguin*. Between then and about 1842, Mocha Dick was said to have been harpooned nineteen times, to have killed more than thirty men, to have attacked three whaling ships and fourteen boats, and to have sunk two merchant vessels. Melville transformed Mocha Dick and his fearsome reputation into *Moby Dick*. The *Penguin* he turned into the *Pequod*. And so Melville resurrected the Mocha Dick of legend as the great white whale of his own immortal *Moby Dick*.

MOCHA DICK:

OR THE WHITE WHALE OF THE PACIFIC: A LEAF FROM A MANUSCRIPT JOURNAL.

BY J. N. REYNOLDS, ESQ.

WE expected to find the island of Santa Maria still more remarkable for the luxuriance of its vegetation, than even the fertile soil of Mocha; and the disappointment arising from the unexpected shortness of our stay at the latter place, was in some degree relieved, by the prospect of our remaining for several days in safe anchorage at the former. Mocha lies upon the coast of Chili, in lat. 38° 28' south, twenty leagues north of Mono del Bonifacio, and opposite the Imperial river, from which it bears w. s. w. During the last century, this island was inhabited by the Spaniards, but it is at present, and has been for some years, entirely deserted. Its climate is mild, with little perceptible difference of temperature between the summer and winter

The story of Mocha Dick, the whale on which Herman Melville based *Moby Dick*, was told in an article titled "Mocha Dick: or the White Whale of the Pacific," published in the *Knickerbocker*, a monthly New York magazine, in May 1839. Above is the first page of the article.

Other Fighting Whales

Timor Jack and New Zealand Tom were other famous fighting whales around that time. Melville had a copy of Thomas Beale's 1839 book, *The Natural History of the Sperm Whale*. Beale described a large whale called Timor Jack who reportedly destroyed every boat that hunted him. In 1804, the crew of the *Adonis* watched as a large whale called New Zealand Tom destroyed nine boats before breakfast off the coast of New Zealand. In *Moby Dick*, Melville refers to them as Timor Tom and New Zealand Jack.

Chapter 4

19th-Century New England Whaling

Before the Civil War (1861–1865), shoemaking and the cotton textile industry were the only industries in New England bigger than whaling. Whaling produced sperm oil, the best fuel for any kind of standard lighting. Spermaceti from the sperm whale's huge head went to make the finest and brightest candles. Lower grades of whale oil were used as lubricants. Articles that needed strength and flexibility (corsets, horsewhips, and umbrella spokes, for example) were made from whalebone. The scarce and expensive ambergris, a substance occasionally found in the intestines of sperm whales, was used to make perfume. More than anything else, however, it was oil that made New England whaling so important. As Melville says in *Moby Dick*, "though the world scouts at [makes fun of] us whale hunters," no matter, because "almost all the tapers, lamps and candles that burn round the globe" burn with whale oil and so "burn, as before so many shrines, to our glory!"

He [the sperm whale] is, without doubt, the largest inhabitant of the globe; the most formidable of all

This advertisement, published in the New Bedford City Directory in 1892, boasts that the corsets sold by the vendors are "warranted all whalebone." The prominence of New Bedford as a whaling town made it the center of various markets for products made of whale oil and whale bone.

whales to encounter; the most majestic in aspect; and lastly, by far the most valuable in commerce; he being the only creature from which that valuable substance, spermaceti, is obtained.

Sperm Whaling

The riches of New England whaling came from hunting not just any old whales, but sperm whales in particular. In the 1600s, Native Americans taught white men how to kill whales from small canoes.

Early Whaling

Until the early 1700s, New Englanders killed mainly humpback and right whales close to shore. In 1712, a Nantucket whaling captain, Christopher Hussey, and his ship were blown far out to sea during a storm. There he came across a school of sperm whales. He killed one and towed it back to Nantucket. This was the first time a Yankee whaler had killed a sperm whale far away from shore. Nantucket whaling ships started to make long-distance voyages around the North Atlantic to kill humpback whales, right whales, and sperm whales. They continued into the South Atlantic to find new whaling grounds.

The first whale ship to take sperm whales in the Pacific Ocean was the *Amelia* (sometimes spelled *Emilia*). It was owned by a famous English whaling company, Enderby & Sons, but was crewed by Nantucketers. In January 1789, the *Amelia* rounded the southern tip of South America. In the Pacific, the crew found sperm whales off the coast of Chile. The ship returned to London with a full cargo of oil. The success of the *Amelia*'s voyage inspired whale ships to head to the Pacific. A few years later, in 1792, two Yankee whale ships, the *Beaver* (out of Nantucket) and the *Rebecca* (from New Bedford), were the first American whalers in the Pacific. The Nantucket whaler *Maro* and Enderby's ship *Syren* discovered the whaling grounds "on Japan" in 1819 and 1820. By the time Melville was born in 1819, sperm whalers were tapping the Pacific Ocean for all the oil it

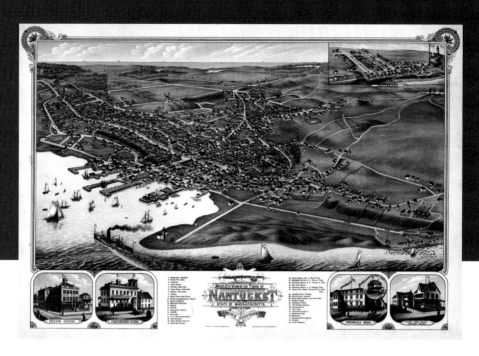

This lithograph gives an aerial view of Nantucket as it appeared in 1881. No longer a whaling center, the town still bore reminders of the days when it was the whaling capital of the world. The cobblestones that pave many of its streets were once used as ballast on returning whalers.

was worth. And the ones doing most of the tapping were the whale ships of Nantucket and New Bedford, Massachusetts.

As most young candidates for the pains and penalties of whaling stop at this same New Bedford, thence to embark on their voyage, it may as well be related that I, for one, had no idea of doing so. For my mind was made up to sail in no other than a Nantucket craft . . . Besides, though New Bedford has of late been gradually monopolizing the business of whaling, and though in this matter

poor old Nantucket is now much behind her, yet Nantucket was her [New Bedford's] great original . . . the place where the first dead American whale was stranded.

Nantucket

The name "Nantucket" is a Native American word meaning "the faraway island" or "land far out to sea." In 1659, two Englishmen living in the Massachusetts Bay Colony, Thomas Mayhew and his son, paid the local Nantucket Indian chiefs £26 (about $40) for the rights to most of Nantucket's land. To turn a profit, they sold those rights to nine other colonists for £30 (plus a couple of new beaver hats for Mr. and Mrs. Mayhew). Later that same year, once all the land rights had been negotiated with the Native American chiefs, the colonists began to settle on Nantucket. The first Nantucket settlers were happy to get away from the intolerant Bay Colony Puritans who particularly disliked Quakers.

Now, Bildad [one of the owners of the *Pequod*], like Peleg, and indeed many other Nantucketers, was a Quaker, the island having been originally settled by that sect; and to this day its inhabitants in general retain in an uncommon measure the peculiarities of the Quaker . . . For some of these same Quakers are the most sanguinary [optimistic] of all sailors and whale-hunters. They are fighting Quakers; they are Quakers with a vengeance.

Nantucketers were converted to Quakerism in the late 1690s. By the early 1700s, Quakers were "the moving force on Nantucket." Nantucket prospered in whaling largely because it was a Quaker community.

> **Whaling demanded an unusual combination of qualities on the part of those followers who would succeed in it . . . courage, hardihood, skill, thrift carried to the point of parsimony, shrewdness, stubborn perseverance, ingenuity, sturdy independence, a cold lack of squeamishness in driving bargains, and a righteous scorn for luxuries. [These Quaker-Puritan values] characterized the Nantucket and New Bedford whalemen who carried whaling to its highest point.**

Nantucket's sandy land was poor for farming. Instead, Nantucketers harvested the sea for their livelihood. The first whale they killed, in the early 1660s, had been stranded in Nantucket harbor. After that, the Nantucketers hunted whales around the shore in small boats.

Offshore Whaling Begins

One day in 1690, a small group of Nantucketers stood on a hill looking out over the sea. They saw, in the distance, the spouts of a school of whales. "There," one man in the group said, "is a green pasture where our children's grandchildren will go for bread." Nantucket's future, in other words, would be harvested not as wheat and bread from its stingy soils but from the blubber and oil of whales in distant seas.

> **And thus have these naked Nantucketers, these sea hermits, issuing from their ant-hill in the sea, overrun and conquered the watery world like so many Alexanders; parcelled out among them the Atlantic, Pacific, and Indian oceans, as the three pirate powers did Poland . . . The Nantucketer, he alone resides and riots on the sea; he alone, in Bible language, goes down to it in ships; to and fro ploughing it as his own special plantation.**

New Bedford

New Bedford, at the mouth of the Acushnet River on the south coast of Massachusetts, was the great rival of Nantucket for its whaling fame. Across the river was its sister port of Fairhaven. By the time Melville wrote *Moby Dick*, New Bedford had overtaken Nantucket as the biggest Yankee whaling port. New Bedford came to the whaling business later than Nantucket, but it earned at least as much fame and fortune from it. By the early 1820s, New Bedford's whaling fleet was about the same size as Nantucket's. By 1842, New Bedford was the biggest whaling port in the world. It would remain so throughout the 1800s.

This photograph, taken by Stephen F. Adams around 1870, shows New Bedford's Central Wharf crowded with casks of whale oil that were unloaded from returning whale ships.

There were several reasons why New Bedford overtook Nantucket in the whaling industry. First, New Bedford manufactured almost everything a whaling ship needed—from ships and boats and rigging, to casks, biscuits, and beef. And when the whale ships returned, New Bedford made candles and other goods manufactured from the whale oil and whalebone they brought back.

You must go to New Bedford to see a brilliant wedding; for, they say, they have reservoirs of oil in every house, and every night recklessly burn their lengths in spermaceti candles.

Originally, Nantucketers also made rigging, provisions, and everything else the whale ships needed. But whale ships got bigger, to make longer voyages. Nantucket was simply too small to provide for their needs.

A related problem for Nantucket was that a sandbar crossed the mouth of its harbor. Bigger ships loaded down with heavy cargoes of whale oil could not get over the shallow bar to enter the harbor. By the 1840s, Nantucket could not compete with New Bedford's advantages.

New Bedford had long gained the upper hand over little Nantucket by the time Melville wrote *Moby Dick*. Still, Ishmael is determined to sail on a "Nantucket craft," out of nostalgia, and because "there was a fine, boisterous something about everything connected with that famous old island, which amazingly pleased me." In that, New Bedford could never compete.

The Golden Age of Yankee Whaling

The golden age of Yankee whaling lasted from the 1830s till around 1850. After the first American oil well was drilled in 1859, crude oil became abundant, more economical, and easier to obtain than whale oil.

Many whale ships were destroyed in the Civil War. In 1871, thirty-four whale ships were crushed in Arctic ice. In 1876, another twelve were lost in the same place. The last whale ship

The crew of the *Charles W. Morgan*, one of the last New Bedford whale ships, is shown cutting into a dead whale on the side of the ship.

to sail out of Nantucket was the *Oak*, in 1869. The last out of New Bedford was the *Wanderer*, in 1924. One of the last New Bedford whale ships, the *Charles Morgan*, can now be visited at Mystic Seaport, in Connecticut.

Chapter 5

A 19th-Century Yankee Whaling Voyage

By the 1840s, most whale ships were three-masted barks. They were small ships, weighing 300 to 400 tons (305 to 406 metric tons) and measuring 100 to 150 feet (30 to 46 meters) long. They were small compared to the big 2,000 to 3,000 ton (2,037 to 3,048 metric ton) cargo sailing ships of the day. Small barks were easy to manage. They needed to be. When most of the crew were out in the boats chasing whales, there were just half a dozen or so "ship-keepers" who stayed on board to sail the ship. Big cargo ships were built to make fast voyages. Whale hunters were built to make long voyages and to fill with whale oil. The *Pequod* in *Moby Dick* was a typical whale ship of the 1840s.

> She was a ship of the old school, rather small if anything; with an old fashioned claw-footed [stubby] look about her . . . Her venerable bows looked bearded. Her masts—cut somewhere on the coast of Japan, where here original ones were lost overboard in a gale—her masts stood stiffly up like the spines of the three old kings of Cologne.

"Fitting Out"

Whale ships had to carry enough equipment and provisions for a voyage that would last from two to four years. Spare rigging, harpoons, pots, knives, miles of ropes and lines, barrels, and a thousand other items were loaded on board. As whales became scarcer, voyages lasted longer.

Food supplies included hundreds of barrels of flour, salt beef, salt pork, salt fish, butter, cheese, beans, fresh water, and many other items to feed a crew of thirty or more for three or four years. The longest whaling voyage on record was nearly eleven years, from May 1858 until April 1869, by the *Nile* out of New London, Connecticut.

The whale ship would spend a few months getting repaired, painted, and generally fitted out for each voyage. Its hull would be inspected for damage. Ships in those days were made of wood. Planks, which rotted over long voyages, had to be replaced. Some ships had thin copper sheets nailed along their bottoms to protect the wood. The sheets had to be replaced from time to time.

Whaling Crews

Whale ship crews were a patchwork of characters and nationalities. In *Moby Dick*, sailors from Nantucket, Holland, France, Iceland, Malta, Sicily, the Azores Islands, China, the Isle of Man, India, Tahiti, Portugal, Denmark, Spain, the Cape Verde Islands,

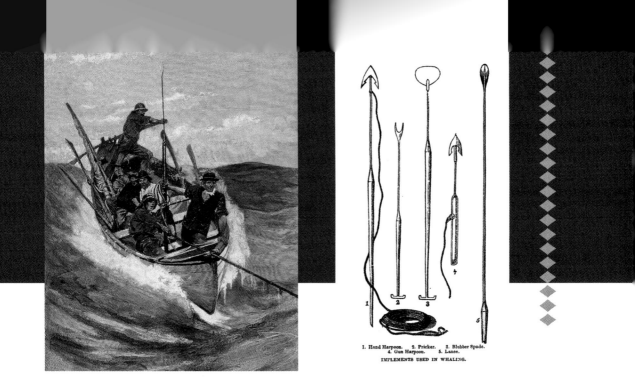

1. Hand Harpoon.   2. Pricker.   3. Blubber Spade.
4. Gun Harpoon.   5. Lance.
IMPLEMENTS USED IN WHALING.

At left, an engraving showing a longboat being pulled by a whale that its crew has harpooned. At right, an illustration of various tools used in whaling.

Ireland, and England are all gathered on the foredeck, "lying in various attitudes, all singing in chorus."

Getting Paid

The crews of whale ships were paid in "lays"—shares of the net profits from the voyage. Ishmael describes the system:

> **I was already aware that in the whaling business they paid no wages; but all hands, including the captain,**

received certain shares of the profits called lays, and that these lays were proportioned to the degree of importance pertaining to the respective duties of the ship's company. I was also aware that being a green [inexperienced] hand at whaling, my own lay would not be very large; but considering I was used to the sea, could steer a ship, splice a rope, and all that, I made no doubt that from all I had heard I should be offered at least the 275th lay— that is, the 275th part of the clear net proceeds [profits] of the voyage, whatever that might eventually amount to.

A captain typically received a lay of 1/12th to 1/18th; a first mate, perhaps 1/25th; and a boatsteerer (harpooner), between 1/70th and 1/100th. Peleg was so impressed with Queequeg's harpooning skill that he offered him "the ninetieth lay [1/90th], and that's more than ever was given a harpooner yet out of Nantucket."

Whatever a sailor bought from the ship's store during the voyage was deducted from his earnings. So were advances of cash made to him before the voyage. The average amount a sailor got at the end of a whaling voyage in the late 1840s was about $5 a month, or about 16 cents a day.

The Whaling Grounds

Once fitted out, the whale ship would set sail for the whaling, or "cruising," grounds. These were stretches of water where

47

whales were most often found. They all had names, such as the Azores Ground near the islands of the Azores, or the Carrol Ground near the island of St. Helena. A whale ship hunting around Japan was said to be "on Japan." The most famous sperm whaling ground was the Offshore Ground in the Pacific, 1,500 to 2,000 miles (2,414 to 3,219 km) off the South American coast, along the equator.

Shipboard Life

In between hunting and killing whales, life on board a whaling ship was quiet, even boring. The crew sailed the ship and, during the day, kept a lookout for whales. They didn't have much else to do.

While the captain had his own cabin, the crew lived together in the forecastle, or fo'c'sle, the small cabin at the front of the ship. J. Ross Browne, a journalist who sailed on a whale ship in 1842, described the fo'c'sle as: "black and slimy with filth, very small and hot as an oven . . . I have seen Kentucky pig-sties not half so filthy." Melville's portrayal of everyday life on a whale ship in *Moby Dick* was highly idealized. He never described the awful living conditions belowdecks.

Nor did Melville mention the crew's revolting food, which ran from bad to disgusting. The crew ate salt beef (often it was actually horsemeat) or salt pork almost every day, twice a day. They also ate hard-as-nails ships biscuits. Sailors always tapped them first to get rid of the weevils.

This 1903 photograph shows crewmen from the ship *Daisy* raising the lower jaw of a whale, exposing its teeth. The inset photograph is of a scrimshaw that was created by a sailor from a tooth of a sperm whale.

The cook sometimes made a "duff" of flour mixed with fat, jam, and raisins, boiled up as a dessert. Lobscouse (or just "scouse") was a hash of crumbled biscuit soaked in the greasy water in which the meat had been boiled.

Ships could not carry much fresh water. The crew drank mostly black bitter coffee sweetened with molasses. The captain and mates had sugar. Occasionally a sailor might catch a dolphin or porpoise, a tuna, or even a sea bird. These were always welcome as fresh food. Sometimes the crew ate whale meat.

To keep themselves occupied, whaling men specialized in something no other seamen did: scrimshaw. They decorated the teeth from the sperm whale's lower jaw by inscribing scenes of life at sea on them. They also decorated whalebone, knife handles, and walking sticks in the same way. The men sometimes made ornamental knots.

"Raising" Whales

Lookouts at the top of the masts kept a constant watch for whales during the day. Whenever a lookout saw the spouts of whales, he called out:

> **"There she blows! there! there! there! she blows! she blows!"**
> **"Where-away?" [meaning, where are the whales?]**

This engraving depicts crew members cutting into a whale. Cutting up a whale to extract its oil and bone was a strenuous exercise that typically involved the whole crew. An adult male sperm whale is about 50 feet (15 m) long and weighs between 77,000 and 110,000 pounds (34,927 and 49,896 kg).

"On the lee-beam [the opposite side of the ship the wind is coming from], about two miles off! a school of them!'"

As soon as the ship "raised [saw] whales," it lowered its boats. A New England whaler usually carried three or four small whaleboats. They were 28 to 30 feet (8.5 to 9.1 meters) long and pointed at each end. Fast and easy to maneuver, they were manned by six men. The mate or the captain commanded each boat and manned the steering oar at the stern. The harpooner, or boatsteerer, pulled the oar closest to the bow to be ready to harpoon the whale when they got close enough.

Whale hunters often rowed several miles to reach a swimming whale. The harpooner at the bow launched his harpoon into the whale to "get fast" to it. If it didn't flip the whaleboat with its tail, the whale would take off at great speed. Often it "sounded" (dove deep). The boat carried 300 fathoms (1,800 feet, or 549 meters) of rope (whale line) attached to the harpoon, to hold onto the whale. The harpooned whale towed the boat so fast that it was called a Nantucket sleigh ride. When the whale tired, the boat could pull in the line and get close to it. Then the boat-header, having changed places with the boat-steerer/harpooner, would plunge a long lance into the whale to kill it. If the boat couldn't get close enough to the whale for the boat-header to get a good shot, he had to throw the lance from a distance.

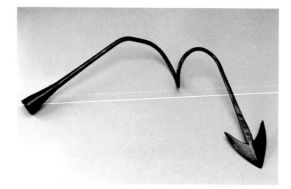

◆◆◆ This twisted harpoon, which dates from around 1820, was retrieved from an unfortunate whale. It offers some clue of the struggle that occurred between the harpooned whale and the boat crew that eventually killed it.

Blubber and Oil: "Trying-Out"

The boat crew had to tow the 50 or 60-ton (45 or 54-metric ton) dead whale back to the ship. That could be ten miles or more away. Some boats got lost and were never found (like the *Rachel's* boats in *Moby Dick*).

The whale was chained to the ship, ready for "cutting-in." The first task was to remove the thick layer of oily blubber covering the whale's entire body. The men stood on a "cutting-stage" rigged over the side of the ship to cut off the blubber in long strips. These long "blanket-pieces" were hoisted on deck and lowered through a hatch to the blubber room below. There they were cut into shorter pieces and sliced into leaves, like a book, called bible-leaves. These were boiled in big pots over brick furnaces on the main deck (the "try-works") to extract the oil.

When the oil had cooled, it was stored in casks belowdecks. A cask contained 31.5 gallons (142 liters) of oil. An average-size sperm whale "tried-out" at nearly fifty casks. A big sperm whale would be up to eighty casks. Any sperm whale that tried-out at more than ninety casks was huge.

The head of the sperm whale was cut off and separated into three pieces: the lower jaw, the "junk" (the lower half of the head), and the "case" (the upper half). The junk was a combination of tissue and spermaceti, while the case was filled with spermaceti alone. The spermaceti was used to make fine candles, while the teeth from the whale's lower jaw were used to make scrimshaw.

A whaling voyage ended when the ship filled up with as much oil and whalebone as it could carry. Back in port, the oil and bone were sold off at market prices. The accounts were drawn up. The men were paid off. If the ship didn't have a full cargo, the cost of the voyage might not be covered.

The End of Whaling

New England whaling declined in the late 1800s. As whales became scarce, voyages became long and unprofitable. Oil from deep below the earth, discovered in America in 1859 by Edwin L. Drake in Titusville, Pennsylvania, would eventually replace whale oil as the fuel of choice for lighting.

The highest point of New England whaling coincided with the writing of *Moby Dick*, one of the peaks of American literature. As fate brought Melville, whaling, and *Moby Dick* together, so circumstances forced them apart. Whaling would die, as did Melville himself, by the end of the century. But "one did survive." Like Ishmael, saved by Queequeg's coffin life buoy, Melville's epic whaling narrative, "owing to its great buoyancy, rising with great force," survived for all time as the immortal *Moby Dick*.

Glossary

ambergris Valuable substance occasionally found in the intestines of a sperm whale; used to make perfume.

blanket-piece A long strip of blubber cut directly from the whale.

boat-header The man who steers the whaleboat chasing the whale and who afterward kills it; usually a mate.

boatsteerer The harpooner on a whaling boat.

case The forehead of a sperm whale, filled almost entirely with spermaceti.

cask The general name for large barrels used on whale ships.

cooper A man who makes barrels, or casks.

cutting-in The process of removing blubber from a whale.

fast To "get fast" to a whale was to harpoon it or to get attached to the whale before killing it.

flukes The horizontal tail of a whale.

foreshadowing Signaling or indicating future events (usually bad) beforehand.

gam A social visit between two or more whale ships meeting at sea.

intolerant Unwilling to let others express their beliefs.

lance A spearlike instrument used to kill a whale.

narrative The details or account of a story, description, or report.

ominous Warning of something bad about to happen.

resurrected Brought back to life.

ship-keepers Men left to sail the whale ship while the boats are chasing whales.

sound To dive, said of a whale.

spermaceti The oily substance within the case and junk of a sperm whale.

splice To combine by interweaving different strands.

stove To smash up a whaleboat, by a whale.

try-pots Huge pots used to boil oil out of blubber.

try-works Brick furnace underneath the try-pots.

whaleboat The boat in which whalemen chase whales

whalebone Whalers' name for baleen, long fibers in the mouth of non-toothed whales; used to make whips, corsets, etc. in eighteenth and nineteenth centuries.

whaler A whaleship.

For More Information

Arrowhead (Herman Melville's home)
780 Holmes Road
Pittsfield, MA 01201
(413) 442-1793
Web site: http://www.mobydick.org

Cold Spring Harbor Whaling Museum
Main Street, PO Box 25
Cold Spring Harbor, NY 11724
(631) 367.3418
e-mail: info@cshwhalingmuseum.org
Web site: http://www.cshwhalingmuseum.org

The Herman Melville Memorial Room at the
    Berkshire Athenaeum
1 Wendell Avenue
Pittsfield, MA 01201
(413) 499-9488
Web site: http://www.berkshire.net/PittsfieldLibrary/lhg/
    melvillerm.htm

Mystic Seaport
75 Greenmanville Avenue and Route 27
Mystic, CT 06355
(860) 572-0711
Web site: http://www.mysticseaport.org

New Bedford Whaling Museum
18 Johnny Cake Hill
New Bedford, MA 02740
(508) 997-0046
Web site: http://www.whalingmuseum.org

Web Sites

Due to the changing nature of Internet links, the Rosen
Publishing Group, Inc., has developed an online list of Web
sites related to the subject of this book. This site is updated
regularly. Please use this link to access the list:

http://www.rosenlinks.com/lal/mobd

For Further Reading

Chase, Owen, et al. *Narratives of the Wreck of the Whale-Ship Essex*. New York: Dover Publications, Inc., 1989.

Dow, Lesley. *Great Creatures of the World: Whales.* Oxford, England: Facts On File, 1990.

Ellis, Richard. *Men and Whales*. New York: Alfred A. Knopf, Inc., 1991.

Francis, Daniel. *A History of World Whaling*. New York: Viking/Penguin Group, 1990.

Hall, Elton. *Sperm Whaling from New Bedford.* New Bedford, MA: The Whaling Museum, Old Dartmouth Historical Society, 1997.

Bibliography

Allen, Everett S. *Children of the Light: The Rise and Fall of New Bedford Whaling*. Orleans, MA: Parnassus Imprints, 1983.

Ashley, Clifford W. *The Yankee Whaler*. New York: Dover Publications, 1991.

Beale, Thomas. *The Natural History of the Sperm Whale*. London: The Holland Press, 1973.

Brown, J. R. *Etchings of a Whaling Cruise*. Cambridge, MA: Harvard University Press, 1968.

Bullen, Frank T. *The Cruise of the Cachalot*. London: Smith, Elder & Co., 1901.

Chase, Owen. *The Wreck of the Whaleship* Essex. San Diego: Harvest/Harcourt Brace & Co., 1999.

Davis, William M. *Nimrod of the Sea, or the American Whalemen*. North Quincy, MA: Christopher Publishing House, 1972.

Hohman, Elmo P. *The American Whaleman*. New York: Longmans, Green & Co., 1928.

Howard, Leon. *Herman Melville: A Biography*. Berkeley, CA: University of California Press, 1951.

Hoyt, Edwin P. *Nantucket: The Life of an Island*. Brattleboro, VT: The Stephen Greene Press, 1978.

Melville, Herman, and Harold Beaver, ed. *Moby Dick: or, The Whale*. Middlesex, England: Penguin Books, 1981.

Olmstead, F. A. *Incidents of a Whaling Voyage*. Rutland, VT: Charles E. Tuttle, 1936.

Philbrick, Nathaniel. *In the Heart of the Sea*. London: HarperCollins, 2000.

Scoresby, W. *An Account of the Arctic Regions with a History and a Description of the Northern Whale Fishery*. Edinburgh, Scotland: Archibald Constable, 1969.

Stackpole, Edouard A. *The Sea-Hunters: The Great Age of Whaling*. New York: J. B. Lippincott Co., 1953.

Vincent, H. P. *The Trying-Out of Moby Dick*. New York: Houghton Mifflin, 1949.

Primary Source Image List

Cover (top): Photograph of Herman Melville, author of *Moby Dick*, taken by Rodney Dewey sometime in the 1860s. Courtesy of Berkshire Atheneum in Pittsfield, Massachusetts.

Cover (bottom left): Photograph, taken by Clifford Ashley in 1904, showing whalers cutting blubber. Housed at the New Bedford Whaling Museum in New Bedford, Massachusetts.

Cover (bottom right): Title page of the first edition of *Moby Dick* by Herman Melville. Published in 1851. Part of the Rare Books and Manuscripts Division of the New York Public Library.

Page 5: *The Spermaceti Whale*, nineteenth-century engraving by William Home Lizars after an original by James Steward. Housed at the Natural History Museum in London, England.

Page 7: Painted portrait of Herman Melville by Asa W. Twitchell. Courtesy of Berkshire Athaneum in Pittsfield, Massachusetts.

Page 9: Portrait of Richard Tobias Green, daguerrotype circa 1845, artist unknown. Housed at the New Bedford Whaling Museum in New Bedford, Massachusetts.

Page 11 (top): *Native of Nukahiva*, drawing by J. A. Atkinson, as published in 1813 in V*oyage Round the World in the Years 1803, 1804, 1805, & 1806*. Housed in the Mariners Museum in Newport News, Virginia.

Page 11 (bottom): Title page of *Typee: A Peep at Polynesian Life* by Herman Melville, published in 1846. Housed at the New York Public Library.

Page 12 (left): Portrait of Elizabeth Shaw. Part of the Gansevoort-Lansing Collection at the New York Public Library.

Page 12 (right): Photograph of Herman Melville's children, taken some time in the late 1850s. Part of the Gansevoort-Lansing Collection at the New York Public Library.

Page 19: *Whale Chart*, map by Matthew F. Maury, 1851. Housed at the Library of Congress Geography and Map Division in Washington, D.C.

Page 26 (left): Title page of *Narrative of the Shipwreck of the Whale-Ship* Essex by Owen Chase, published in 1821. Part of the Rare Books and Manuscripts Collection at the New York Public Library.

Page 26 (right): Undated photograph of Owen Chase. Housed at the Nantucket Historical Association Research Library in Nantucket, Massachusetts.

Page 33: Page from the article "Mocha Dick: or the White Whale of the Pacific," published in the *Knickerbocker* in May 1839. Part of the Rare Books and Manuscripts Collection at the New York Public Library.

Page 35: Advertisement for corsets made from whalebone. Published in the New Bedford City Directory in 1892. Housed at the New Bedford Whaling Museum in Massachusetts.

Page 37: *Bird's Eye View of the Town of Nantucket*, lithograph, published by J. J. Stoner in 1881. Housed in the Library of Congress Geography and Map Division in Washington, D.C.

Page 41: Photograph of casks of whale oil at Central Wharf, New Bedford. Taken by Stephen F. Adams around 1870. Housed at the New Bedford Whaling Museum in Massachusetts.

Page 49: Photograph of crew raising a whale on the whale ship *Daisy* in 1903. Taken by Dr. Robert Cushman Murphy. Housed at the Nantucket Historical Association in Nantucket, Massachusetts.

Page 49 (inset): Scrimshaw created by an unknown sailor between 1850 and 1860. Housed at the Mariners' Museum in Newport News, Virginia.

Page 52: Twisted harpoon from the early nineteenth century. Housed at the New Bedford Whaling Museum.

Index

About the Author

Graham Faiella writes mainly nonfiction books and articles on subjects related to the sea. He is originally from Bermuda and has lived in the United Kingdom since 1974.

Photo Credits

Cover (top) Rodney Dewey, Berkshire Athenaeum, Pittsfield, Massachusetts; cover (bottom left), pp. 9, 35, 41 courtesy of the New Bedford Whaling Museum; cover (bottom right), pp. 26 (left), 33 courtesy of the Rare Books and Manuscripts Collection, New York Public Library Astor, Lenox, and Tilden Foundations; p. 5 Natural History Museum, London, UK/ Bridgeman Art Library; p. 7 Asa Twitchell, Berkshire Athenaeum, Pittsfield, Massachusetts; p. 11 (top) General Research Division, New York Public Library Astor, Lenox, and Tilden Foundations; pp. 11 (bottom), 49 (inset) The Mariners' Museum, Newport News, Virginia; p. 12 (left and right) courtesy of Gansevoort-Lansing Collection, New York Public Library; p. 17 J. W. Hill, *View, New York, 1848—From St. Paul's Chapel, Broadway & Fulton St.,* 1848, Museum of the City of New York, The J. Clarence Davies Collection; pp. 18, 23 © Bettmann/Corbis; pp. 19, 37 Library of Congress, Geography and Map Division; pp. 20, 22, 46 (left), 51 © North Wind Picture Archives; pp. 26 (right) (GPN4448), 43 (F4987), 49 (top) (F1051T), 52 (S8023) courtesy of the Nantucket Historical Association; pp. 43 (F4987), 49 (top) (F1051T), 52 (S8023) Courtesy of the Nantucket Historical Association; p. 46 (right) Library of Congress, The Nineteenth Century in Print: Periodicals Collection.

Design: Les Kanturek; Editor: Jill Jarnow;
Photo Researcher: Rebecca Anguin-Cohen